Brown v. Board of Education of Topeka

Challenging School Segregation in the Supreme Court

Jake Miller

The Rosen Publishing Group's

PowerKids Press™

New York

Published in 2004 by The Rosen Publishing Group, Inc.
29 East 21st Street, New York, NY 10010

First Edition
Editor: Jennifer Landau, Frances E. Ruffin
Book Design: Emily Muschinske

Photo Credits: Cover and title page, pp. 5, 5 (inset) © Carl Iwaski/TimePix; p. 6 © Rischgitz/Hulton/Archive/Getty Images; p. 8 © Hank Walker/TimePix; p. 8 (inset) Library of Congress, Prints and Photographs Division; p. 9 Topeka Schools Collection, Kansas Collection, Spencer Research Library, University of Kansas; p. 11 © Joseph Scherschel/TimePix; p. 12 © Gordon Parks/TimePix; p. 15 © Margaret Bourke-White/TimePix; p. 15 (inset) © Shel Hershorn/TimePix; pp. 16, 19 © Bettmann/CORBIS; p. 19 (inset left) © Topeka State Journal, courtesy of the Kansas State Historical Society; p. 19 (inset right) NARA—Old Military and Civil Records; p. 20 (inset) © Associated Press; p. 20 © A.Y. Owen/TimePix; p. 22 © CORBIS.

Front cover: Linda Brown, third child from the left, and classmates line up outside their classroom.

Miller, Jake, 1969–
Brown v. Board of Education of Topeka : challenging school segregation in the Supreme Court / Jake Miller.—1st ed.
    p. cm. — (The library of the civil rights movement)
Includes bibliographical references and index.
  ISBN 0-8239-6250-4 (library binding)
1. Brown, Oliver, 1918—Trials, litigation, etc.—Juvenile literature. 2. Topeka (Kan.). Board of Education—Trials, litigation, etc.—Juvenile literature. 3. Segregation in education—Law and legislation—United States—Juvenile literature. [1. Brown, Oliver, 1918—Trials, litigation, etc. 2. Segregation in education—Law and legislation. 3. African Americans—Civil rights.] I. Title: Brown versus Board of Education of Topeka. II. Title.
  KF228.B76 M55 2003
  344.73'0798—dc21
                                        2001007238

Manufactured in the United States of America

Contents

A Little Girl's Big Court Case

In 1951, Linda Brown was a seven-year-old second grader in Topeka, Kansas. Linda lived a few blocks away from an elementary school, but every day she walked across dangerous railroad tracks to catch a crowded bus to a school on the other side of town. She wasn't allowed to go to the school in her neighborhood, because it was just for white children, and Linda was African American. Making people of different skin colors use different schools or other public places is called **racial segregation**. Linda's father didn't think segregation was fair. With the help of a civil rights group called the National Association for the Advancement of Colored People (NAACP), Linda's father came up with a plan. He tried to **enroll** Linda in her neighborhood school. When he was turned away, he filed a **lawsuit** against the Topeka **Board of Education**.

This picture shows Linda Brown and her family. Inset: Linda, age 10, and her 6-year-old sister walked along the train tracks to catch the bus to a segregated school.

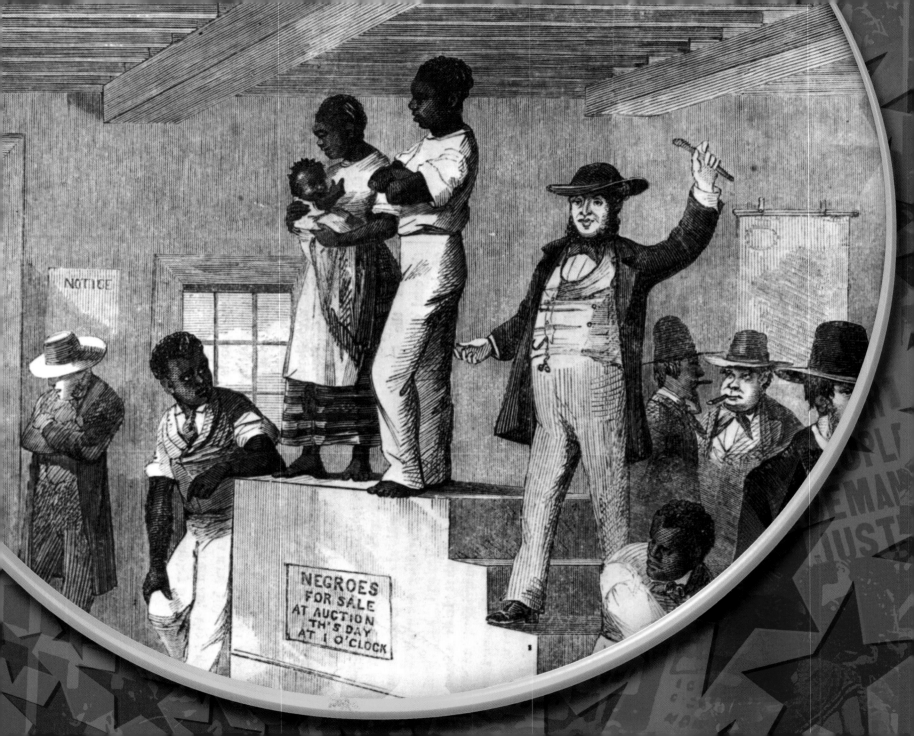

Unequal Treatment

During the 1700s and the 1800s, black people in America had very few rights. Many blacks were slaves who were treated like property, not like people. They could neither vote nor own their own homes. Southern **plantation** owners depended on slave labor, while many people in the North wanted to abolish slavery. Tension about this issue was one cause of the **Civil War**, which lasted from 1861 to 1865. Near the end of the war, slavery was **abolished** by the Thirteenth **Amendment** to the U.S. **Constitution**. The North won the war, and in 1868, **Congress** passed the Fourteenth Amendment. It stated that all Americans were equal in the eyes of the law. In reality blacks and whites were still treated differently. Blacks had to obey special laws, called Jim Crow laws, that stated where they could live, work, and go to school.

Slaves were auctioned, or sold, at slave markets. Black families were often broken up when family members were sold to different plantations.

Then and Now

In 1896, the U.S. Supreme Court made a "separate but equal" ruling that led to segregated schools. In 1954, a U.S. Supreme Court decision overturned this policy, desegregating America's public schools.

Fighting for Black Rights

Linda Brown's father was not the first black person to file a lawsuit against the Jim Crow laws. In a famous case in 1896 called *Plessy v. Ferguson*, the U.S **Supreme Court** ruled that it was legal to make black people ride in different train cars from white people, as long as the different train cars were similar in quality. This policy was called separate but equal. Cities such as Topeka, Kansas, used this ruling to **justify** sending Linda Brown and the other black students to separate schools.

The NAACP worked hard to make life better for black people like Linda Brown. The group had been founded in 1909 to fight unfair laws and violence against African Americans.

Before the separate but equal ruling, some schools in Topeka, Kansas, were integrated, like this classroom.

 Black segregated schools were often inferior. In 1953, the boy in this picture had to take time out from his schoolwork to add wood to a fire that kept his class warm. Inset: The soda machine was labeled Whites Only.

9

An Equal Education

The NAACP fought hard to help blacks get the right to a good education. Often that meant fighting to get blacks into schools that were open only to whites. The leaders of the NAACP thought the fight for equal education should start with schools for adults, such as colleges. They started their fight with adult education, because the idea of sending black and white children to the same school made many whites angry. Starting in the 1930s, the NAACP won some important cases. These victories let blacks attend all-white law schools, like the one at the University of Texas. The courts said that having different schools for blacks and for whites was illegal if the schools were not of equal quality. If there wasn't a good graduate school, such as a law or a medical school, for blacks to attend, then they could attend a white graduate school.

Herman Marion Sweatt was the first black man to attend classes at the once all-white University of Texas law school.

A Divided School System

The NAACP saw that segregated schools for black students like Linda Brown were often much worse than schools for white children. Most white kids went to school in sturdy brick buildings and had plenty of books. Black kids had classes in falling-down shacks and had no school supplies. Some school districts spent three times as much money on their white students as on their black students. The NAACP also believed that separate schools made black children feel that they weren't good enough to go to white schools. Many white people were **prejudiced** against blacks. A large number of whites thought black children were not as smart as white children were. They feared that if black and white children went to school together, it would lower the quality of the white children's education.

This is not a photograph of a classroom from the 1800s. It is a picture of a classroom at a school for black students in 1956.

All the Way to the Supreme Court

To protest school segregation, the NAACP took on Linda Brown's case, along with cases from school systems in Delaware, Virginia, South Carolina, and Washington, D.C. These cases were all tried in court as *Brown v. Board of Education of Topeka*. The schools for blacks in Linda's hometown of Topeka, Kansas, weren't as bad as were black schools elsewhere, so it was important to prove that segregation itself was harmful to African American children. The NAACP's lawyers found scientific studies that showed that black children in segregated schools started to believe the prejudices that others held against them. The lawyers argued that to undo this damage, black and white students should attend the same schools. The NAACP took the fight to end school segregation all the way to the U.S. Supreme Court.

This 16-year-old boy supported segregation. He lost his eye while protesting integration in public schools. Inset: Daniel Carey, a Dallas, Texas, minister, lied to people in his church. He said that the Bible supported segregation.

STATES RIGHTS

Then and Now

During the 1950s and the 1960s, some white groups protested against desegregation with violence. Today several states are making laws against hate crimes.

Arguments in Court

Thurgood Marshall and the other lawyers at the U.S. Supreme Court who represented the segregated school districts argued that the idea that blacks and whites were equal in the eyes of the law was never meant to force blacks and whites to attend the same schools. They argued that the idea of separate-but-equal schools should be respected. They also said that local communities should be allowed to run their own schools without interference from the national government. Members of the **Justice Department** worried that segregation was starting to make the United States look bad to other countries. The U.S. Constitution stated that the United States stood for fairness and for equality. It was hard for countries around the world to believe that when they saw how badly African Americans were being treated in the United States.

Thurgood Marshall was the lead attorney for the Brown *case. In 1967, he became the first black associate justice, or judge, of the U.S. Supreme Court.*

17

The Supreme Court Decides

After the U.S. Supreme Court heard all the lawyers speak in *Brown v. Board of Education of Topeka*, the judges asked both sides to provide more information. It took two years from the start of the trial for the Supreme Court to rule. On May 17, 1954, the court finally decided to overturn the separate but equal **policy** and to declare school segregation illegal. Many people celebrated this decision as a great step toward equality and freedom. During the next 25 years, the Supreme Court made many decisions that protected the rights of black people and of other Americans facing **discrimination**.

Thurgood Marshall stands with other lawyers outside the U.S. Supreme Court after winning the Brown v. Board of Education of Topeka *case. Inset: This is the official Supreme Court judgement and a newspaper headline announcing the decision.*

Attacks and Shutdowns

Although Linda Brown and the NAACP won an important legal victory, there were still many problems to overcome before real progress was made in the schools. Southern states, where most of the laws on segregation were in effect, did everything that they could to stop black children from entering white schools. Angry mobs of white people threatened and attacked black people who tried to integrate schools.

In 1957, the governor of Arkansas had soldiers from his state's national guard keep blacks from entering a high school in Little Rock. President Dwight D. Eisenhower had to call out the U.S. Army to protect the black students. Some states gave white children scholarships so they could attend white-only private schools. Other states simply shut down all of their public schools for the year so that blacks and whites wouldn't have to attend school together.

Dwight Harrison of Houston, Texas, shown with his father, Charles, and Ruby Bridges (left) *of New Orleans attended newly desegregated schools.*

21

The Struggle Continues

The fight for equal rights for blacks continues today. Linda Brown, the schoolchild at the center of *Brown v. Board of Education of Topeka*, went back to court as an adult in the 1990s. This time she was fighting for her own children's rights to attend integrated schools. Topeka still had schools that were mostly black, and schools that were mostly white. More than 40 years after the *Brown* decision, Topeka opened three new schools that were designed to help balance the mix of students. The *Brown* decision remains a symbol that represents the hope and the promise of the Civil Rights movement. Linda Brown won more than just the right to go to school in her neighborhood. She won the right to believe that she was truly an equal citizen.

National guardsmen are called in to uphold integration at a school in Little Rock, Arkansas.

Glossary

abolished (uh-BAH-lisht) Done away with.

amendment (uh-MEND-mint) An addition or a change to a constitution.

board of education (BORD UHV eh-juh-KAY-shun) A group of people who run a town's school system.

Civil War (SIH-vul WOR) The war fought between the northern and southern states of America from 1861 to 1865.

Congress (KON-gres) The part of the U.S. government that makes the laws.

constitution (kahn-stih-TOO-shun) The basic rules by which a country or a state are governed.

discrimination (dih-skrih-muh-NAY-shun) Treating a person badly or unfairly just because he or she is different.

enroll (en-ROHL) To make or to become a member.

Justice Department (JUHS-tis dee-PART-mint) The part of the U.S. government that enforces the laws of the land.

justify (JUS-tuh-fy) To show to be fair.

lawsuit (LAW-soot) A case in a court of law where one side argues against another in front of a judge.

plantation (plan-TAY-shun) A very large farm. During the 1700s and the 1800s, many planation owners used slaves to work on these farms.

policy (PAH-lih-see) A law that people use to help them make decisions.

prejudiced (PREH-juh-dist) Deciding on a belief without knowing the facts.

racial (RAY-shul) Having to do with a certain race of people.

segregation (seh-gruh-GAY-shun) The act of separating people of one race, gender, or social class from another.

Supreme Court (suh-PREEM KORT) The highest court in the nation.

Index

Web Sites

To learn more about *Brown v. Board of Education of Topeka* and the Civil Rights movement, check out this Web site:
http://civilrightsmuseum.org/tour/index.html

Primary Sources

Cover: Linda Brown (third from left). By Carl Iwasaki. **Page 5:** Linda Brown and her family. By Carl Iwasaki. **Page 5** (inset): Linda Brown and her sister. By Carl Iwasaki. **Page 6:** Print of an American slave auction. (1861). From the Rischgitz collection of Hulton Archive. **Page 8:** A Public school for black students in Virginia. (1953). **Page 8** (inset): Soda machine labeled "White Customers Only!" (1943–1960). From the Library of Congress. **Page 9:** Monroe School in Topeka, Kansas (1892). From the University of Kansas Libraries. **Page 11:** Herman Sweatt at University of Texas Law School (1950). By Joseph Scherschel. **Page 12:** Sub-standard classroom for black students (1956). By Gordon Parks. **Page 15:** Young segregationist. By Margaret Bourke-White (1956). **Page 15** (inset): Texas Minister Daniel Carey. By Shel Hershorn (1964). **Page 16:** Attorney Thurgood Marshall (1955). **Page 19:** Attorneys Marshall and Nabrit at the U.S. Supreme Court (1954). By Bettmann. **Page 19** (inset left): Topeka State Journal, May 17, 1954. From Kansas State Historical Society. **Page 19** (inset right): Supreme Court judgement (1955). From National Archives and Record Administration. **Page 20:** Charles Harrison and son. By A.Y. Owen. **Page 20** (inset): Ruby Bridges integrating school in New Orleans. **Page 22:** U.S. National Guard enforcing the law in Little Rock (1957).